THE STORY OF COMPUTERS

It is only forty years since the first computers were built. Their history is the story of man's search for better ways to write, count and communicate. Computers now form a vital part of our lives and affect all aspects of our society. Their story is an exciting one and an important one.

Ian Litterick is an expert on microcoputer systems, a writer and an inventor. Chris Smithers has wide experience in illustrating computers. Both author and designer share an interest in helping nonexperts to understand, and so to control, computer technology.

The Age of Computers

THE STORY OF COMPUTERS

Ian Litterick
Designed by Chris Smithers

The Bookwright Press
New York · 1984

Other books in this series

Computers in Everyday Life
How Computers Work
Computers and You
Robots and Intelligent Machines
Programming Computers

First published in the United States in 1984 by
The Bookwright Press, 387 Park Avenue South, New York, N.Y. 10016

ISBN 531–04775–X

First published in 1983 by
Wayland (Publishers) Limited
49 Lansdowne Place, Hove,
East Sussex BN3 1HF, England

Library of Congress Catalog Card Number 83–72810

Printed in Italy by G. Canale and C.S.p.A. Turin

Contents

In 1999

School in 1999. The class sits facing its tutor. On the wall is a large screen showing a picture like a television picture. But the screen is completely flat and only sticks out the width of a thin book from the wall.

"Today," the tutor said, "today, as you know, we are going to have a history lesson. The history of the computer to be specific. Who was it that invented the computer? Well, it is difficult to know exactly who it was. What do we mean by 'a computer'?"

"Would anybody like to give me a definition?"

"A computer is a machine for organizing and changing information," recited Tamara, who was slightly bored.

"OK," said the tutor, "let's look at the ways in which a computer can organize information. What sort of things can you do with a computer?"

"Mine stores a lot of information," said Helen, who usually spoke up first.

"I do calculations with mine," Tom called out.

"I use mine for writing my school work," said John, who often tried a bit too hard to keep on the right side of the teacher.

"I use mine for typing things into," said Sandy.

"Mine presents information to me according to the criteria which I stipulate," said Larry, who was rather pompous.

"I write programs on mine," said Tamara, who had just finished building her voice-controlled bedside alarm system.

Right and opposite *School in 1999.*

"I send messages with mine," said Hazel, who had a pen-pal in Japan. She spent most of her pocket money writing to him by computer.

"I only play games on mine," joked Larry, who held the record for the highest score on the school's microbic invaders game.

"Fine," replied the tutor. "You are all

right, of course. The invention of the computer is the story of all these things – of storing information, of calculation, of writing, of typing, of presenting information, of programming, of sending messages and of playing games. And no doubt there are other ways of looking at it, too. But we'll start with one of the ones you have suggested. Which one would you like to choose?"

A list of the topics was displayed as a menu on the screen at the front of the class, and each of the children selected a button on their computer pads and pressed it. The tutor quickly added their choices together, and started to talk and to show pictures. This is what the children learned.

Writing through the ages

Nobody knows where writing started. Did our ancestors first scratch with their fingers in the earth to point a direction, or did they use a stick of charcoal to tally the day's kill?

Writing has been very important in setting mankind apart from other animals. By writing knowledge down we can transmit it to people in other places and in future times. No longer are we limited to getting information from and giving it to the people that we personally know. We can communicate with anyone who can understand our written marks.

We know that people were drawing pictures of bison on the walls of caves in Lascaux, southern France, 30,000 years ago. But we do not know what they meant. They may only have been to persuade the gods to help them hunt, or to give thanks for good hunting.

The Egyptians were writing with pens made of reeds 4,000 years before Christ. They wrote on papyrus – a writing

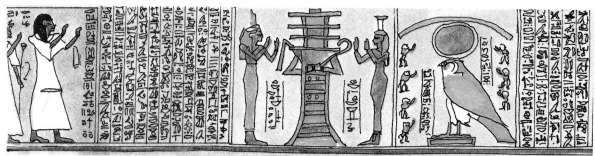

Top *Part of a cave wall painting.*
Above *An example of early Egyptian hieroglyphics.*
Right *Some Japanese* Kanji *characters.*

material made from rushes – and this has given us our word for paper. They also wrote by carving on the walls of their burial chambers and on stone slabs. They used a system of writing called hieroglyphics. Instead of making words up from individual letters, as we do with our alphabetic system, each word is represented by a kind of picture.

In 1,000 B.C., the Chinese were using brushes of camel's and rat's hair to write with. To this day, they use a system of writing where each word is represented by its own complicated pictogram or character. The Japanese use the same system, which they call *Kanji*. This makes it very difficult to use computers for processing their writing.

The quill pen, made from goose, swan or turkey feathers, was used from the sixth century B.C. until the nineteenth century A.D., when metal nibs took its place. Quill making was a skilled task and at one time thirty million quills a year were being imported into Britain.

L. E. Waterman, an American, produced the first practical fountain pen in 1884. But its reign was comparatively short, as a Hungarian, Lazlo Biro, managed in 1944 to make a ball-point pen which really worked. Felt-tipped pens came into favor during the 1960s.

"So where do computers come in?" asked Tom. "They haven't taken over from ball-point pens. Look, I still have a ball-point pen . . ." He fished around in his bag looking for it. ". . . somewhere," he said.

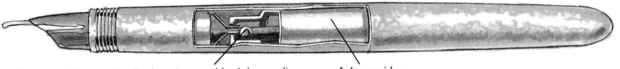

Sealing ball (pushed back when the cartridge is inserted)   *Ink cartridge*

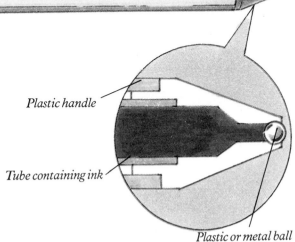

Plastic handle

Tube containing ink

Plastic or metal ball

Top *A modern fountain pen.*
Above *A ball-point pen and a cross-section through the ball point.*
Left *An eighteenth-century quill pen.*

Printing and typewriters

If writing was important in allowing mankind to develop its intelligence, then printing was doubly so. Before the invention of the printing press, knowledge and science remained in the hands of a small number of people who had access to books.

Above *A thirteenth-century monk preparing an illuminated manuscript.*

All books had to be written by hand, and a scribe could reproduce only a small number of books in a lifetime. So books were very rare and only the rich could afford them. Few people had the opportunity to learn to read.

The Chinese had started printing as early as A.D. 200. They used carved wood blocks containing whole pages of words and pictures, which they printed on paper. Later they used separate blocks for each word, so that they could be used again and again.

Paper reached the West from China in the twelfth century. This made printing easier, but printing itself did not reach Europe from China, and so had to be reinvented.

In Europe there was already some printing from wood blocks before a German, Johannes Gutenberg, invented the printing press in about 1450. But it is his press which is usually regarded as the beginning of printing.

We do not know whether Gutenberg really invented the printing press, or whether he just put together other people's ideas. One such idea was for casting type, so that each individual letter – "C," for example – was cast from the same mould as the other letter "C's." The individual letters were then arranged in racks of type.

Another idea was to use a press for the actual printing. This squeezed the type firmly down onto the paper, giving a

Right *An individual letter of cast type and the rack in which cast type is assembled into words.*
Middle *Gutenberg and his assistant making printed sheets.*
Bottom *A nineteenth-century printing press.*

much sharper impression than the previous methods of smoothing the paper down onto the printing block. Gutenberg put these two elements together and started a printing revolution.

Printing developed quickly from then onward, and many different techniques were used for printing books, newspapers and pictures.

A large number of inventors put their minds to making a machine which could write in such a way that it looked as if it had been printed. C. Latham Sholes, of Milwaukee, Wisconsin, was not the first person to invent a typing machine, or typewriter as it later became known. But he was the first person – in 1867 – to make one which actually worked, and could be sold commercially.

Sholes's machine had letters of type on the ends of bars, arranged in a circle. When you hit a key on the keyboard a type bar would fly up to hit the underside of a roller which had paper around it. It made an impression on the paper through an inked tape. You could only see which letter had been struck by picking up the roller.

Within a few years, Sholes's machine was made by the Remington Company, which had previously made guns and sewing machines. In many ways the typewriter is more the true predecessor of today's computers than the calculating machines from which the

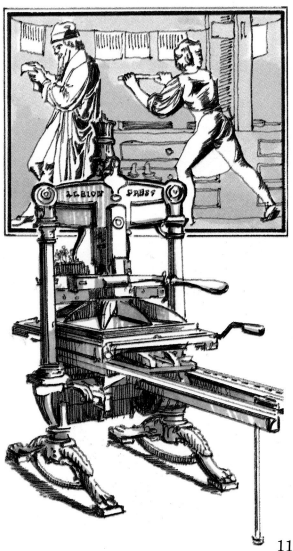

computer is more directly descended.

In one respect, Sholes has left his mark on practically every computer that is used today – the QWERTY keyboard. Have you ever wondered why the keys are in this particular order on so many keyboards?

Sholes had trouble with his typewriter. If he pressed one key too quickly, before the previous type bar had fallen back, the two keys would jam. This was especially likely to happen if the two keys were next to each other in the circle. So Sholes changed the layout of his keyboard, which had originally been in alphabetical order. Now, keys which were often struck one after the other came from opposite sides of the circle in his machine.

The QWERTY layout was not designed to make it easy to type. The last thing that Sholes was worried about was enabling people to type quickly. His only concern was to make his machine work at all!

Many early typewriters had two keyboards – one for small letters and the other for capitals. It was not until typists were trained to touch-type that it was proved that it was faster to use one

Above *Layout of the QWERTY keyboard.*
Right *A Remington typewriter of 1907.*
Below *Sholes's typewriter of 1873.*

keyboard and a shift key.

By 1890 the arrangement of the type bars had changed, so that they now came up to strike the paper from the front. This had the advantage of allowing the typist to see the characters as they were being typed.

Thomas Edison invented an electric typewriter as long ago as 1872, but very few were used in offices. Instead, it developed into the ticker-tape machine, which is used for receiving and transmitting messages.

It was not until the 1920s that electric typewriters became available for use in offices, and not until the 1950s and 1960s that they became common. They were easier to use than manual typewriters.

The golf-ball typewriter was introduced by International Business Machines (IBM) in 1961, and allowed the style of type to be changed by changing the "golf ball." The same mechanism was used as a printer on some computers.

The daisy-wheel, originally used in computer printers in the 1970s, is now used on typewriters. The distinction between typewriter and computer printer is fast disappearing.

Left *An IBM golf-ball typewriter.*
Above *A daisy-wheel computer printer.*

Calculating

The usual way of telling the story of computers is to trace the history of mathematical calculation. The direct forerunners of our computers were designed for one purpose only – to calculate.

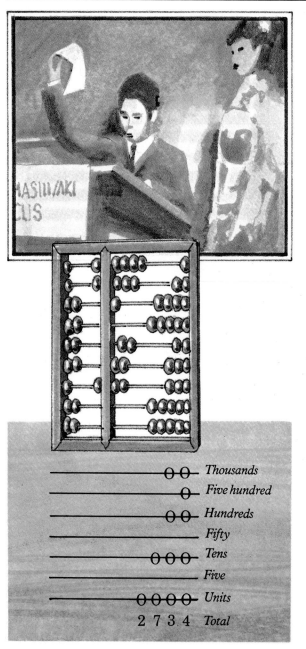

		Thousands
		Five hundred
		Hundreds
		Fifty
		Tens
		Five
		Units
2 7 3 4		Total

The only information that the early computers dealt with was numbers. The things that we mostly use computers for today – processing words, storing facts, keeping records, teaching, and controlling machinery – came later, almost as an accidental by-product of the need to count and calculate.

It was many thousands of years ago that people started to count. But until our ancestors settled down to farm the land and then started to trade and barter – one pig for a neighbor's five flint axe heads, for example – they had little need to count.

A stick with notches cut in it was the only calculator that early man needed. Such tally sticks were in use in Europe until the last century.

The first machine for calculating was the abacus. It was used in China over 5,000 years ago and is still in use in some parts of the world today.

Different countries use different kinds of abacus, but they all have a number of

Top *Kiyoshi Matsuzake used an abacus to win an arithmetic contest. His opponent used a desk calculator.*
Middle *A common form of abacus.*
Bottom *Calculating numbers using an abacus.*

beads which can be pushed along rods to mark the intermediate results of calculations. Skilled users can calculate very quickly using an abacus. There was a celebrated competition shortly after the Second World War between an American, Thomas Wood, who used a calculator, and a Japanese clerk, Kiyoshi Matsuzake, who used an abacus. The abacus won, but the calculator had been given to someone who couldn't operate it very well, so the contest was a bit one-sided!

Perhaps the first attempt to bring science to the aid of calculation was in the early seventeenth century, when a Scotsman, John Napier, invented logarithms. In this system, multiplication and division can be carried out by adding and subtracting, not the number itself, but a related number – the logarithm. He also invented a system of sticks (called "Napier's bones," because they were made of bone or ivory), which could be used as an aid to multiplication and division.

Although much more simple, Napier's bones were the forerunner of the slide rule, which for a long time was an essential tool for mathematicians. The slide rule suddenly disappeared in the 1970s, when the pocket calculator arrived to do everything that it could do, and much more.

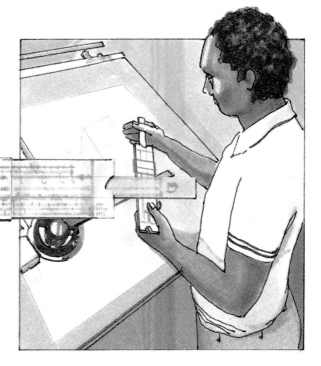

Top *John Napier and his ingenious device known as "Napier's bones."*
Right *Until very recently, the slide rule was an indispensable tool for making calculations.*

In 1642 the French mathematician and philosopher, Blaise Pascal, produced an adding machine. It used a train of cogs to add numbers in the same way that a mechanical odometer or mileage indicator works today. A computer programming language has been named after Pascal, but his Pascaline, as the machine was known, was not widely used.

Next we go to Germany, where another mathematician and philosopher, Gottfried Leibniz, invented a more complex reckoner some thirty years later. It also used toothed wheels, but this machine could also multiply and divide by adding or subtracting repeatedly.

Machines based on the same principles as Leibniz's are still in use as mechanical adding machines today, although most have now been thrown out in favor of electronic calculators.

"Well," said the tutor, "we have covered about 27,000 years of the history of calculating and there are only 300 left to go. So perhaps we'll have a break now. But first, does anybody know the nationality of the next person in our story, Charles Babbage, who was the first person to design a general-purpose computer?"

"Chinese," said Melinda. "The Chinese invented most things, it seems – paper, printing, calculating. So I expect they invented computers as well."

"They didn't," replied the tutor. "Charles Babbage was an Englishman, the son of a banker."

Above *Blaise Pascal and his adding machine.*
Below *Gottfried Leibniz and his calculating machine.*

Babbage's amazing Analytical Engine

Until the 1790s, the calculating machines which had been invented were only designed to carry out a limited range of calculations. Charles Babbage was the first person to design a general-purpose machine.

Babbage, who was born in England in 1791, is known as one of the major founders of computing. It is strange that he should have this reputation, for he never actually got his machines to work!

His first machine was called a Difference Engine. It was designed to calculate the tables for logarithms which Napier had invented 200 years before, and which were now increasingly important at the beginning of the Industrial Revolution.

Babbage was concerned that it took a person a long time to make the calculations necessary to produce a log table, and mistakes in the tables were common. If he could design a machine to do calculations, humans would be spared that tedious chore, and the results would be more reliable.

So he persuaded the British Government to give him some money to build his engine. It was based, like those before it, on systems of cogs and levers, but was much more complex. Babbage even intended that it should print out the results at the end right onto paper.

But with the skills and technology of the time it was impossible to

Left *Charles Babbage and part of his Difference Engine.*

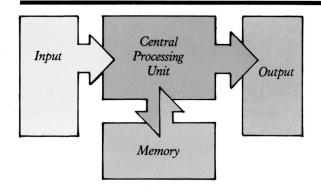

Left *The essential parts of a computer system.*
Below *The Countess of Lovelace.*
Bottom *Part of Babbage's Analytical Engine.*

manufacture the various cogs, wheels, rods and levers accurately enough to enable it to work reliably. In 1833, after spending the huge sum for that time of £17,000 ($25,500 today), he gave up.

Undaunted, he started dreaming of an even grander machine – one which would not just perform one task, but which could be made to do an infinite variety of different calculations. In short, it would be flexible and it would be programmable. He called this his Analytical Engine, and he planned to use a steam engine to drive it!

Babbage's idea had all the essential parts of the modern computer – input; a central processing unit, which he called the "mill"; storage for intermediate results, which we would call "memory"; a control unit to make the machine perform its calculations in the right order; and output in the form of a printer.

We know about the details of Babbage's machine because he was befriended by Ada Augusta, Countess of Lovelace, a mathematician and the daughter of the poet, Lord Byron. She talked to Babbage about his proposal and made copious notes describing it.

But it was never built. Babbage was far ahead of his time and his writings were lost until 1937. Computers had to wait another hundred years, and they would never be powered by steam.

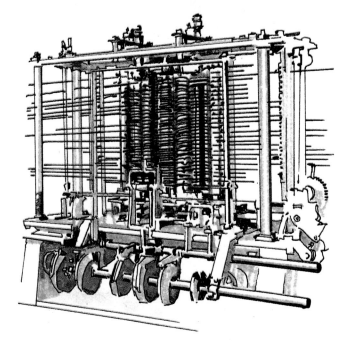

Birth of the punched card

Inventors should be broad-minded, as ideas often come from the most unlikely of places. One of the most important ideas in early computing came from weaving – the punched card.

Perhaps the oldest and truest slogan about computers is GIGO – short for Garbage In, Garbage Out. It is very important to feed the correct programs and the correct data into your computer, otherwise what comes out is sure to be wrong.

It was the weaving industry which gave Babbage a solution to the problem of ensuring reliable input.

In the early 1800s, Joseph-Marie Jacquard, a Frenchman, invented a loom for weaving. This loom was controlled by linked wooden cards with holes in them. The cards were drawn through the loom as it wove, and each set of holes controlled one movement of the loom.

In order to weave the thread into different patterns, weavers had to move individual rods to control the spools of thread of different colors. Jacquard saw that this task could be done equally well by allowing a card with holes in it to control the movement of the rods. The holes allowed some rods to pass through, while the solid parts stopped the others.

Looking at each set of holes as a number, Jacquard had invented the principle of numerically controlled machinery – still in use today – and the

Top to bottom *Portrait of Joseph-Marie Jacquard, some Jacquard "punched" cards, and a Jacquard loom in use.*

concept of punched card and punched tape for computer input. The name of Jacquard still survives in the computer world as the name of a computer manufacturer.

An American statistician, Herman Hollerith, made commercial use of Jacquard's ideas in processing the results of the U.S. census of 1890. It had taken so long to process the results of the 1880 census by hand, that the Census Bureau decided it had to make some radical changes. The Bureau held a competition to find a way of dealing with the census more effectively. Hollerith easily won with his tabulating machine.

Details about each citizen were punched onto stiff paper cards, each position on the card signifying a different piece of information. The cards

Top *Herman Hollerith and a Hollerith punched card (above left).*

Left *Hollerith's tabulating machines in use. The inset (above) shows the cards being punched.*

could be read at high speed aided by the new power of electricity. Several different pieces of information could be counted at the same time, thus allowing the different statistics to be easily compared with each other.

Within six weeks of the 1890 census, the total population of the U.S. had been calculated to be 62,622,250. Hollerith's system was an instant success, and he set up the Tabulating Machine Company to make and sell the machine.

Direct descendants of the machine, using similar principles, are still in use today, and Hollerith's code is still used to code modern punched cards.

In 1911 Hollerith's company merged with two other companies to form the Computing, Tabulating and Recording Company. By the time he died in 1929,

this company had changed its name to the International Business Machines Corporation. Better known as IBM, it is now the world's largest computer company.

Of course, there were many other people whose ideas contributed to the development of computers, and George Boole was one of them. In 1859 he formulated the concept which we now know as Boolean algebra. He showed how, by using only two states – 0 and 1, or true and false, or on and off – you can create a system which enables machines to make logical decisions. Digital computers could not work without it, and we shall soon be coming to them.

But first let's look at how computers have developed as machines for sending messages.

Above *An early IBM electric punched card machine.*
Right *Thomas J. Watson, the man who brought IBM into the computer age.*
Far right *A picture of an early IBM office.*

Sending messages

We need to be able to send each other messages in order to organize our modern lives and run our society. The message which a computer sends in an instant could have taken a year to deliver before the invention of telecommunications.

Above *In the nineteenth century, the telegraph system of sending messages became widespread. Telegraph wires often ran alongside railroad tracks.*

For many, many years the only way that people could send each other messages was by getting somebody to take them – either by word of mouth, or by letter.

Signal systems have also been around for a long time. When the weather provided enough visibility, people sent each other messages by smoke signals, by waving flags or by flashing lamps.

Early civilizations, like the Romans and the Incas, had elaborate networks of signal stations stretching across their countries. And they needed to be elaborate, for each link could only stretch as far as the eye could see.

Postal systems developed from private, message-carrying services, but were very expensive until Rowland Hill started the penny post in 1839. His British postal service carried a letter anywhere in the country for one penny and was the first cheap and truly public postal service.

Telegraph systems developed during the middle of the nineteenth century. Their wires often ran alongside railroad tracks and they sent coded messages – using a system of flags or displays, or Morse code. Morse code is a system invented by Samuel Morse for sending the letters of the alphabet. Each letter has a code made up of short and long sounds – dots and dashes.

Only after Alexander Graham Bell invented the telephone in 1876, did it become possible to send the sound of the human voice itself over wires by electricity. Although Bell's technique was not the only possible one, he managed to get a patent – No.174,465 – which effectively stopped anybody else from offering a telephone service in the United States.

Bell recognized that a telephone service would be commercially useful when other people could not see that it had any value. He did the work necessary to set up a proper telephone network. Within ten years there were 150,000 telephone users with 1,180 exchanges and 235,000 km (146,000 miles) of telephone wires in the U.S. alone.

These networks soon spanned the world. Radio links via satellites were added in the 1970s and 1980s, and the telephone system provided the basis for the computers' telecommunications networks.

Top *The letters of the alphabet as represented by the dots and dashes of Morse code.*
Right *The changing shape of the telephone.*

A.–	H....	O–––	V...–
B–...	I..	P.––.	W.––
C–.–.	J.–––	Q––.–	X–..–
D–..	K–.–	R.–.	Y–.––
E.	L.–..	S...	Z––..
F..–.	M––	T–	
G––.	N–.	U..–	

The Gower-Bell telephone of the 1880s had two listening tubes

A 'candlestick' telephone of the 1900s

A 'cradle' telephone of the 1930s

'Intelligent' telephones of the 1980s have an internal memory and can call often-used numbers at the press of a button.

23

The first computers

A lot had changed between Babbage's time and the 1930s. Mechanical calculators had become commonplace, but there was still no general-purpose Analytical Engine or computer such as Babbage had proposed.

It is easy, when telling the story of one particular part of our lives, to lose sight of everything else that is changing. Since our story began, even since Babbage had his dream, the world had changed. By the 1930s, it had become a radically different place.

Most of the Western world now lived in towns and cities. Most people made their living directly or indirectly from industry. The world had become much more complex, much more man-made.

Motor vehicles, sea and air transportation, and the telephone had made the world a smaller place. Everybody in the Western world now went to school, and most people could now read and write. Electricity reached into practically every home.

It was electricity which finally made Babbage's ideas into a reality. The computer was an idea whose time had finally come. Indeed, so true was this that in at least three different countries people were simultaneously working to build the first modern-day computing devices.

Conrad Zuse, a young German engineer, built what was probably the first of these machines. In 1936 he started to build a model mechanical

Top *The Z1 in the living room of Zuse's family home.*
Middle *Instructions for the Z2 machine were punched into old 35mm film.*
Right *Conrad Zuse at work on one of his machines.*

Below *A German Enigma code machine. During World War II, computers were used to break the codes of such machines.*

computer, basing it mainly on the construction toy, Meccano. The Z1, as he called it, took over his family home as it grew. It used the binary system, which enabled him to take advantage of Boole's system of logic. Like today's computers, it had a keyboard for putting the numbers into the machine. Zuse claimed not to know anything about Babbage's work, which was not surprising as Babbage had been forgotten. Z1 showed that Zuse's ideas worked and he started to make Z2.

In Z2 he replaced the slow, mechanical switches that he had used on Z1 with electrical relays similar to those being used for telephone switch gear. He also speeded up the input by using old 35 mm film with holes punched in it, in just the same way that paper tape would be generally used for computers later.

Zuse went on to build Z3 and Z4 during World War II. Fortunately, Adolf Hitler did not take up his suggestion that these computers would be ideal for deciphering coded messages sent by the enemy.

In England, however, it was for just this purpose that the first work on computers was carried out. The work was so secret that it was many years before details of it started leaking out.

The Polish secret service had managed to steal from the Germans one of their code machines, called Enigma, so the Allies knew how the German code system worked. But they did not know the keys to the code, because the keys

Right *Alan Turing, one of a group of people who designed Colossus.*
Below *A vacuum tube and the codebreaking computer, Colossus.*

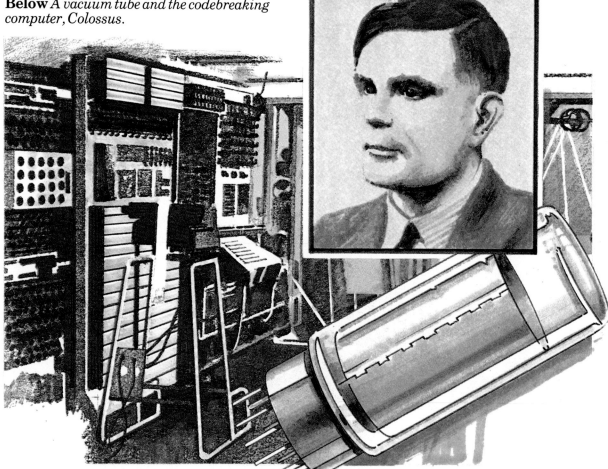

Right *Alan Turing, one of a group of people who designed Colossus.*
Below *A vacuum tube and the codebreaking computer, Colossus.*

were regularly changed. In a country house called Bletchley Park, a small group of people worked at developing machines to crack the German codes. They included Alan Turing, who was a mathematician. He had written a paper – *On computable numbers* – before the war, showing how the ideas of Boole could be used in computers.

They put together a number of machines using electric relays and fed information in on punched paper tape at the rate of 2,000 characters a second. But this was not fast enough. So they decided to speed things up and put together another machine called Colossus. They used electronic valves,

or vacuum tubes, which can switch on and off thousands of times a second, compared with the ten or so times a second of an electric relay.

Invented by Sir William Crooks, an Englishman, in the mid-eighteenth century, vacuum tubes had been developed and improved over the years and were starting to be used in electronic equipment like radios. The tubes gave out a lot of heat and were very unreliable. Colossus had some 2,000 tubes, and as each tube had a life of only 1,000 hours or so, early computers were always breaking down. But Colossus worked, and it worked very fast, so before the end of the war

Below *The Harvard Mark I and its designer, Howard Aiken.*

ten others were built.

But while these were the first electronic computers, they do not qualify as the first general-purpose ones. All they could do was work at the one task of breaking codes. To change their program, their wiring had to be rearranged – not something their operators wanted to do very often.

Meanwhile, in America, another mathematician, Howard Aiken of Harvard University, had been reading Babbage's work. He thought he could make a modern version of Babbage's Analytical Engine. He talked to Thomas J. Watson, by then the dynamic and iron-willed boss of IBM, which was now very successfully selling mechanical calculators. Aiken persuaded Watson to put up a million dollars to finance the Automatic Sequence Controlled Calculator, which he continued to work on when he was drafted into the Navy. Better known as the Harvard Mark I, it was switched on in 1943.

It was an enormous machine, clad in streamlined metal 15 meters (50 feet) long, and 2.4 meters (8 feet) high. It also used electric relays, and so was very slow compared with the fully electronic machines which were to follow closely on its heels. But it worked and put the name of IBM in the forefront of the computer business.

The first generation

World War II, as we have seen, stimulated a lot of the early work on computing – just as military needs have accounted for a lot of the research effort since then.

J. Presper Eckert and John W. Mauchly, of the University of Pennsylvania, developed ENIAC during the last part of the war. Completed in 1946, the Electronic Numerical Integrator And Calculator, to give it its full name, was designed to calculate quickly the ballistic course of shells.

With 19,000 tubes it was a huge machine, and needed the output of a small power station to feed it with electricity. It worked 1,000 times faster

Left *J. Presper Eckert holding part of a unit from ENIAC.*
Below *The ENIAC computer in operation.*

than a machine using electric relays, and could do in two hours nuclear-physics calculations which it would have taken 100 engineers a year to do by hand. Unlike most computers since then, it worked on the decimal system, rather than working in binary.

The program could be changed by rewiring a panel – so it was a true general-purpose machine – but this was still a very laborious task.

Most of the early computer pioneers were mathematicians, as in those days it was necessary to understand mathematics when building computers from the smallest logic components. One such mathematician was John von Neumann, who was working on the atom bomb project.

He became involved with ENIAC because such a machine would be useful to check his own calculations. He had the original idea that a computer could not only store data and intermediate results, but that it could also store a program. That way the program could be read in fast, like the data. A program could call up other programs and even modify itself as often as needed – thousands of times faster than a human operator was capable of doing.

Von Neumann's ideas have been the foundation of the design of computers ever since. Numbers are used to code the programs and so to control the computer. The computer has several different arithmetical functions built in.

IBM started to sell a machine called the 701 in 1953. At this time, a number of computers were built in Britain – in Manchester and Cambridge, among other places. Computers started to be used in business. But they remained very expensive to make and to run. It seemed as if ordinary people would never use them.

Below *UNIVAC (Universal Automatic Computer), one of the first commercial computers, went into service in 1951.*

The transition to transistor

It was still to be some years before the computer would be liberated – taken away from the white-coated high priests who served it – and put in the hands of ordinary people to use.

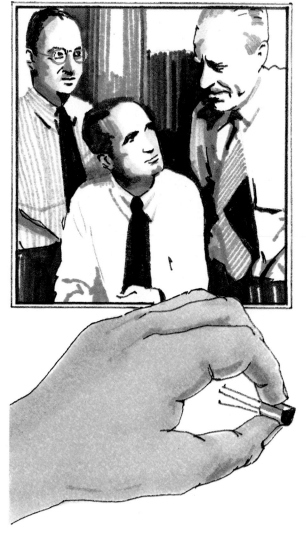

An essential step in liberating the computer was the invention of the transistor. In 1948, John Bardeen, Walter H. Brattain and William B. Shockley discovered what they called the "transfer resistor" – shortened to transistor – in the laboratories of Bell Telephone, the company which ran most of the American telephone system. They were working with materials called semi-conductors, which are halfway between insulators like rubber, wood and ceramic, and conductors like steel and copper.

By mixing very small quantities of particular impurities with the semi-conductors, they made a little switch which would control the passage of electricity. The switch itself was operated by a small electric current. It could be used like a relay but with no moving parts, and it had many advantages over the vacuum tube:

- It worked like a tube, but very much more reliably.
- It took up a thirtieth of the space of a tube.
- It used a twentieth of the electricity.
- It created and wasted a fiftieth of the heat.
- It soon cost less to make and within forty years would cost one-hundred thousandth of the price.

Top *From left to right, Bardeen, Brattain and Shockley, joint inventors of the transistor.*
Above *One type of modern transistor.*

Above *An IBM System 360 computer. It was introduced in 1964.*

It would bring a revolution perhaps as far-reaching as the invention of the wheel or the automobile. And certainly the revolution was to happen far quicker.

Bardeen, Brattain and Shockley were jointly awarded the Nobel Peace Prize in 1956 for their invention.

A second generation of computers appeared during the late 1950s and 1960s using transistors. Although faster, smaller and more powerful than their forerunners, they were still expensive monsters which only large organizations could afford to use.

In the early 1960s, IBM confirmed its position as world leader with the 360-series of computers. Other companies, like Univac, came along behind. Still others grew, but failed to keep up with the rapid advances in the technology, and so went bankrupt or were taken over.

Apart from IBM, the firms which had dominated the office equipment market were slow to realize the importance of computers: that computers would actually replace most other office equipment.

The integrated circuit

During the 1960s, the twin contests of the space race and the arms race caused the United States to spend huge sums of money on developing computers. Much of the effort went into trying to make them smaller.

When the transistor was discovered, it was a logical step to combine a number of transistors together. Other elements, apart from transistor switches, are needed to make logic gates – the basic elements which computers use to make decisions. The main ones are resistors, which make it difficult for the electricity to pass through a circuit; and capacitors, which store electricity for a short time.

Instead of having one transistor on its own, several transistors could be integrated with the other components and sealed up in a small package. The package was called an Integrated Circuit (IC) or, more popularly, a chip.

The primary ingredient of a chip is silicon, which is just purified sand, one of the commonest elements known to mankind. Once manufacturers had invested in chip-making machinery, the cost of a chip became very low – they

As computers diminished in size, they also became more powerful:
Left *Part of a computer made in 1949.*
Below *A transistorized circuit board of the 1960s.*

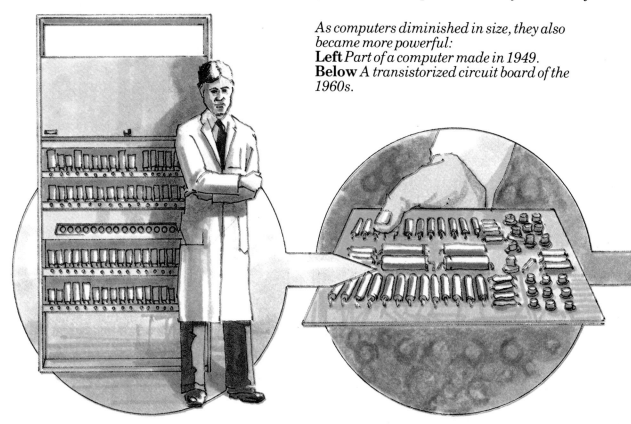

could be made in thousands by a process rather like developing a photographic film.

In the race to put men on the moon, the United States started off with a handicap compared with the U.S.S.R. – U.S. rockets were much smaller. It was vital to use computers widely to control the spacecraft, to navigate and to give information to the astronauts and to mission control about what was happening in the craft. But computers were big and heavy.

So the American space scientists had to make up with miniaturization what they lacked in rocket power. Their computers had to shrink. The result was that more and more components were put onto a single chip. By the early 1970s, chips like the Intel 8008 and 4004, which contained the whole of a central processor, were commercially available – the microprocessor had arrived.

This was certainly a great advance, but the first microprocessors were only simple computers. They were suitable for controlling machinery, rather than for doing all the information processing and calculation work which we expect from a full-fledged computer.

Computer memory, too, was put on to silicon chips. For much of the early days, computers had used magnetic cores for memory. These were tiny little rings of magnetic material, which had to be strung together on wires like beads. They were expensive to make, slow in use, and quite bulky.

Memory chips were more reliable and faster, and stored at first a few hundred, and then later many thousands of bits of memory on one piece of silicon 5mm (0.2 in) square.

Below *A typical memory chip of the 1980s.* **Right** *The American space program encouraged the design of small computers.*

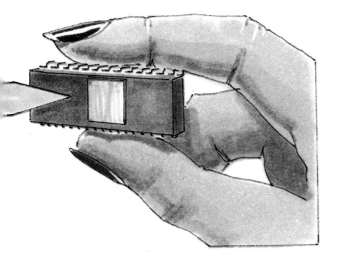

The mini revolution

Computers had been getting bigger, faster and more powerful. Now, thanks to the transistor and the new integrated circuits, they got smaller and cheaper. This affected the way computers could be used.

From the earliest days of the computer, there had been experiments with small machines. In 1951 an experimental small machine, called the Whirlwind, had been built at the Massachusetts Institute of Technology (M.I.T.) in Boston. It was even faster than most computers of the time – so fast that it could be used to control machinery.

Most computers at this time were used for batch processing – all the input programs and data were fed into the machine together at the beginning of a computer run, and then, some moments later, all the results came out as output. While the computer was running, nothing could be changed. But to be able to control machinery, a computer needs to be able to interrupt its program to respond to new information fed to it by the sensors connected to the machine. It must be able to do this very quickly, before the information changes again. This is called "real time" processing.

Below *A drilling machine controlled by a minicomputer.*
Below right *Whirlwind, the forerunner of the modern minicomputer.*

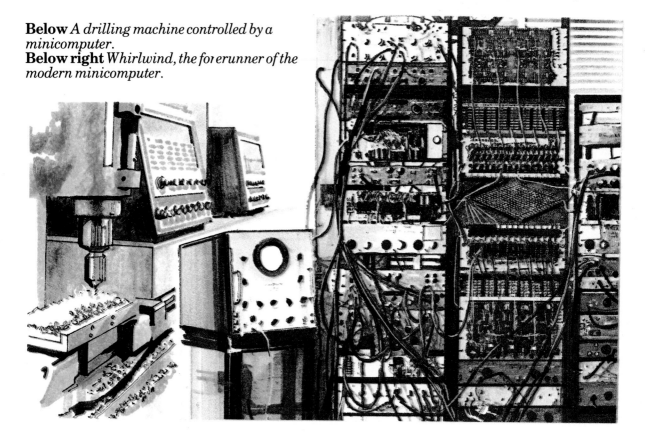

The Whirlwind led to the TX-0, a computer which was built in 1953, again at M.I.T., using transistors. It was used to test memory cores.

In 1957 Kenneth Olsen, who had been working on these projects at M.I.T., left to form his own computer company, the Digital Equipment Corporation (DEC). This made a number of computer logic boards, and then in 1959 produced a complete small computer called the Programmed Data Processor-1(PDP-1). It cost $120,000, a very low price for a computer in those days.

Computers like this became known as minicomputers. They were comparatively small and cheap, and tended to be programmed and operated by the people who were using them, rather than by specialist programmers and operators. But it is difficult to draw an exact line between a mini and its larger relative – the mainframe.

In 1965 DEC produced the PDP-8, which became a workhorse throughout the world. In 1968, when a new version was built using integrated circuits, it only cost $13,200. By using such small and comparatively cheap machines it was possible to have a number of local computers, rather than a single large central computer.

Minicomputers like the DEC PDP series were adopted by scientists in laboratories and used to control machinery in factories. They were also used in businesses to run accounting programs and to provide information for management. They became very widely used.

Below *A minicomputer system of the 1970s.*
Below right *A DEC PDP minicomputer system.*

The dawn of the micro

Computers were still surrounded by a lot of mystery. But in a few places there grew up groups of hobbyists who lashed together bits of old computers and some of the new components when they could get them.

Above *Early personal computers were available as kits.*

A company called MITS (Micro Instrumentation and Telemetry) of Albuquerque, New Mexico, had sold a number of electronic construction kits, including one based on the Intel 8008 chip. By late 1974, Intel had developed a more advanced microprocessor chip called the 8080. Ed Roberts, President of MITS, designed a computer based on the 8080.

Popular Electronics magazine published an article about this computer, which it called the Altair 8800, in the January 1975 edition, and the article mentioned that the computer would soon be available as a kit for only $395.

It was a computer which one person

Monitor

Disk drives

Printer

could afford and one person could use – the first personal computer.

As a single 8080 chip cost $350 at that time, 2,000 orders for the computer came flooding in when MITS still had only one prototype. However, they managed to make more, and had sold 8,000 computers by the end of 1975.

The original Altair came with just 1k – one thousand characters – of memory. Quite soon other firms started to build their own printed circuit boards to add on to the Altair – for attaching terminals, video screens, and printers to it.

By the end of 1976, there were about six different firms making computers of the same kind, some of them starting to

use the more powerful Z-80 chip. Over 30,000 microcomputers were sold in 1976, practically all in the United States. The personal computer was here to stay.

The groups of computer hobbyists were particularly strong on the West Coast in one part of California. The area was known as Silicon Valley because of the large number of companies there which were involved in making silicon chips.

One day in 1976, a couple of young men turned up at one of the groups with something that they had put together in their garage.

It used one of the new 8-bit micro-processor chips (a Mos Technology

6502), which enabled them to put together a complete computer: a keyboard for input, a processor, a few thousand characters of memory, and the means to connect it up to a screen to see the results. And it all fitted in one small box. They had designed it because they could not afford the Altair.

They called the machine the Apple I, and they started selling it ready-made, not as a kit. They soon realized that they had stumbled, almost by mistake, on a gold mine. Their little box could be made very cheaply – at a fraction of the price of any proper computer before then.

Steve Wozniak and Steve Jobs, as the young men were called, made 200 Apple I's, and sold them easily. They went on to design and build the Apple II, and put it on sale in 1977 at a price which brought it within the range of people who could afford a fairly expensive hi-fi set. Because it was ready-built, it appealed to a whole new range of people who did not know about electronics or computers.

Until 1976, even personal computers had only been suitable for experts. But now computers like the Apple II could reach ordinary people.

A couple of other firms found themselves making microcomputers almost by accident. A Tandy Corporation engineer decided that he could make a microcomputer, and was given permission to do so. The TRS-80 was announced in 1977 and became an instant success.

Commodore Business Machines – which

Top to bottom *Three computers for personal use: a Tandy TRS-80; a Commodore PET; and an IBM microcomputer.*

made calculators – put together the Personal Electronic Transactor, or PET, and this, too, was a success. When it became clear that it was businesses, not home users, who were buying it they changed its name to the CBM computer. But the name PET stuck.

People who worked with traditional mini and mainframe computers were scornful of the new microcomputers, calling them "toys." Of course, they had originally been introduced largely as playthings. It was the users, the people in businesses and schools, who had seen that they were true computers and could be used seriously.

Slowly, the traditional computer people started waking up to what was happening under their noses. They started to realize that these new micros were often better and had better programs than their larger forerunners.

They started producing cheaper and cheaper machines themselves, and in 1981 the computer giant, IBM, produced its own personal computer, thus giving the seal of approval to the microcomputer.

The IBM personal computer was also one of the forerunners of a second generation of more powerful microcomputers. They used the new 16-bit microprocessors, which enabled them to run much faster and to use huge amounts of memory. The micro was now as powerful as a mini of only ten or so years before.

Below *The micro is now as powerful as a minicomputer of only ten years ago.*

The language of computers

Programming computers – getting them to do what you want them to do – is quite difficult. The task is made easier by a good programming language. Programming languages have developed over the years as much as computers themselves.

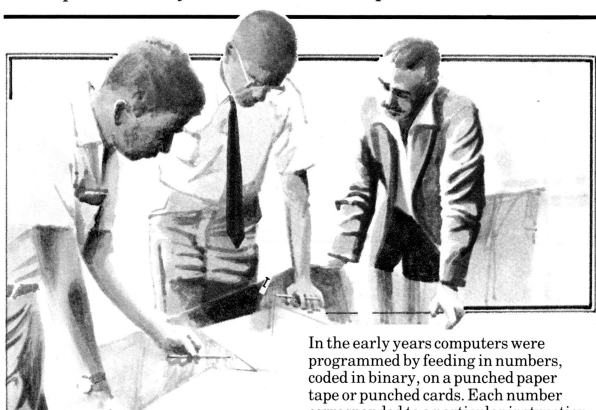

Above *Thomas Kurtz (middle) and John Kemeny (right), the designers of BASIC – the first language to be used on microcomputers.*

In the early years computers were programmed by feeding in numbers, coded in binary, on a punched paper tape or punched cards. Each number corresponded to a particular instruction to the computer. This system of instruction is called machine code.

It is difficult to remember what all the codes mean (there may be several hundred of them). So a system of mnemonics was invented, so that the letters DAA, for example, would replace the number 27. This was called assembler language, because the letters are "assembled" by the computer into numbers.

01000111011011110110111101100010
00100111011011000011011010111111

Left *A short example of machine code (top),*
and a BASIC program.

Below *Part of an assembler program.*

```
10  PRINT "Welcome to programming"
20  PRINT "What is your name?"
30  INPUT N$
40  PRINT "Goodbye," N$;
50  PRINT "That's all I do."
60  END
```

0800	476F6F	GD BYE	DB
	646279		
	6524		
1000	210008	MSGPRN	LXI
1003	7E	WRTMES	MOV
1004	FE24		CPI
1006	C8		RZ
1007	23		INX
1008	4F		MOV
1009	E5		PUSH

Even with these mnemonics, writing programs was still laborious, so languages were devised, known as high-level languages, which allowed programs to be written in words and symbols close to ordinary English.

Between 1954 and 1956, IBM produced Fortran (FORmula TRANslator) aimed at making mathematical and scientific programming easier. COBOL (COmmon Business Oriented Language) followed for business use, together with a number of other languages (ALGOL, LISP, PL1, for example), each with its own particular advantages.

BASIC (Beginners' All-purpose Symbolic Instruction Code) was designed by Professors Kemeny and Kurtz at Dartmouth College, New Hampshire. They wanted a language that could be easily learned and yet would be versatile. It made it possible for ordinary people to learn how to use computers. BASIC was the first language to be used on microcomputers.

In 1975, Bill Gates and some friends in Seattle, Washington, wrote a version of BASIC for the Intel 8080 chip to run on the Altair. This was very successful and immediately established BASIC as the language for microcomputers.

Pascal was devised by Niklaus Wirth in 1971 to help programmers write more accurate programs. It was named after Blaise Pascal, inventor of the calculating machine. It quickly became popular, influenced the way BASIC developed, and also became widely used on microcomputers.

In the late 1970s, the U.S. Defense Department specified a new language, called Ada (after Charles Babbage's friend Ada Augusta), which incorporated most of the improvements in Pascal, but was very complex.

Back in 1999

The tutor drew the series of lessons to a close. Most of the rest of the story had happened in the children's lifetime, so it wasn't really history to them.

"You know most of the rest of the story," it said. "You have got the results of the next generation of microcomputers on your desks. Which reminds me, perhaps I should have mentioned Sinclair.

"In the early 1970s, Clive Sinclair of Cambridge, England, had designed and built the smallest and cheapest calculator available at that time. It had sold in large quantities until the Japanese came along with even smaller and cheaper ones a couple of years later.

"Sinclair soon turned his mind to computers, and in 1980 produced the ZX-80, a tiny computer which could be linked up to a television set and which sold for the unbelievable price of about $200. A year later he even improved on this with the ZX-81, which was cheaper still and had only four chips.

"In a way that was the forerunner of your school computers: it was compact, and mass-produced so that it was very cheap. Although it, too, was regarded as a toy, people started using it for serious purposes, like controlling machinery and even as an office computer. The ZX-81 was followed by other increasingly powerful, but very cheap, computers.

"Then, of course, the Japanese came into the microcomputer market, and miniature flat screens were developed.

Voice input also came at this time, which enabled us to talk directly to the computer.

"And that is the story of the computer, or at least one version of it. Because, of course, I have selected some parts to tell you and left out others. But now is the time to hand you back to your teacher . . ."

There was an undignified scramble as the children at the front of the class dived for the tutor's power plug to pull it out while the tutor was still speaking. It had become a tradition in the class, which for some reason their teacher, sitting at the back of the classroom, turned a blind eye to. As it always did when its plug was pulled out, the automatic tutor's voice rose to a comic squeak and the screen dissolved into a bright mass of shooting stars and went blank. The lesson was over.

Left *Clive Sinclair and his ZX-80 and ZX-81 microcomputers.*

Below *Back to the school classroom in 1999.*

Glossary

Binary Counting to base two.

Bit The smallest unit of information, a 0 or a 1 in the computer.

Byte A byte is made up of eight bits. A megabyte is one million bytes.

Capacitor An electronic component which holds electricity for a period.

Cast To make a metal object by pouring molten metal into a mold.

Central Processing Unit (CPU) The area of the computer where the main information processing is carried out.

Circuit A collection of electric or electronic components having wires or links between them. An integrated circuit has all these components and links on one silicon chip.

Conductor Something which conducts electricity.

Daisy-wheel A removable print element in some printers.

Data The information which a computer deals with.

Decimal Counting to base ten.

Digital Working in digits or numbers.

Electronic A term used to refer to equipment which uses components like transistors and vacuum tubes to control the current.

Gate A component, made up of transistors, which will produce a particular logical result.

"Golf ball" A small, removable metal sphere around the surface of which the characters of type are arranged.

Input The information which is put into a computer.

Insulator A material that does not conduct electricity.

K A symbol for the numeral 1024.

Lever A bar which pivots and can be used for moving objects.

Logic A system of reasoning where a particular set of inputs will predictably produce a particular set of outputs.

Mainframe A large computer.

Microcomputer A computer based on a microprocessor. While a microcomputer usually means a complete microcomputer system with input, output and storage, the word is sometimes used for the actual microprocessor chip.

Microprocessor A term which is usually used to mean the single chip containing the central processing unit, but it can also be used to mean the complete microcomputer system.

Minicomputer A computer midway between a micro and a mainframe in size.

Mnemonics Technique of using a word or words to trigger memory.

Odometer An instrument that measures and records the distance that a vehicle has covered.

Output The results which come out of a computer after processing.

Pad A pad, or keypad, is an array of switches for inputting data. A digitizer pad is a writing tablet for putting writing or lines into the computer.

Processor The part of the computer where the processing is done. If the processor is on a single chip it will be called a microprocessor.

Program Instructions which are written into a computer to make it work.

Prototype An early version of a machine, built to experiment with and to see how well it will work.

Relay A switch operated by electricity. Unlike a transistor, a relay has moving parts.

Resistor A component which resists the passage of electricity.

Satellite Something which revolves around something else. Usually this refers to man-made devices orbiting the Earth, which are often used for communicating or transmitting information.

Scribe A person who makes hand-written copies of a document or book.

Sensor A device for sensing something that is happening – for reading changes in temperature or light levels, for example.

Shift key A key on a typewriter used to adjust the action of the machine so that it types capital letters.

Silicon Silicon is purified sand. It is the raw material of integrated circuits.

Slide rule A mechanical calculating device using the same principles as logarithm tables.

Statistician Somebody who calculates and classifies tables of figures.

Telecommunications The science of communication by telephone, telegraph, radio and television.

Ticker tape Paper ribbon used for printing telegraphed messages.

Transistor An electronic component which can be used as a switch. It has no moving parts.

Tube A vacuum tube.

Vaccuum tube An electronic valve or thermionic valve in the form of a vacuum-filled glass tube which can be used as an amplifier or as a switch.

Wood block A method of printing whereby the inked face of a carved wooden block is pressed down onto paper.

Finding out more

Books

You may want to start finding out more about computers by reading the other books in this series:

Computers in Everyday Life tells how we will be using computers in our daily lives.

How Computers Work explains what the different parts of a computer do and how they are made.

Robots and Intelligent Machines is about computers at work and on the move.

Programming Computers talks about the languages we use to get computers to work for us.

Ardley, Neil. *Computers*. New York: Warwick Press, 1983.
——. *Using the Computer*. New York: Franklin Watts, 1983.
Baldwin, Margaret and Pack, Gary. *Computer Graphics*. New York: Franklin Watts, 1984.
Berger, Melvin. *Data Processing*. New York: Franklin Watts, 1983.
Bitter, Gary G. *Exploring With Computers*. New York: Messner, 1981.
D'Ignazio, Fred. *Invent Your Own Computer Games*. New York: Franklin Watts, 1983.
Graham, Ian. *Computer Games*. Tulsa, Oklahoma: EDC Publishing, 1982.
Herda, D. J. *Microcomputers*. New York: Franklin Watts, 1984.
Lampton, Christopher. *Programming in BASIC*. New York: Franklin Watts, 1983.

Lipson, Shelley and Stapleton, Janice. *It's BASIC: The ABC's of Computer Programming*. New York: Holt, Reinhart and Winston, 1982.
Lorsen, Sally G. *Computers for Kids: Apple II Plus Edition*. Morristown, N.J.: Creative Computing, 1981.
Mintz, Martin and Mintz, Sandra. *Computers in Our World, Today and Tomorrow*. New York: Franklin Watts, 1983.
Van Horn, Royal. *Would You Like to Be a Computer Scientist?* Plainfield, Illinois: Unica, 1982.

Magazines

There are a number of general magazines about microcomputers, in which people sometimes write about the way computers are affecting our lives. They include *Byte, Computing Today, Creative Computing, Interface Age, Microcomputing,* and *Personal Computing*.

For people who have a particular microcomputer, there are also many magazines which deal with individual popular models.

Computers

You can also use computers to find out about computers.

Computerized Bulletin Boards are spreading in several countries. Your computer talks to another computer over the telephone, and you can look at messages and feed games and programs onto your own computer.

Index

Index